IGNATIAN EXERCISES
CHARISMATIC RENEWAL

SIMILARITIES ? DIFFERENCES ?
CONTRASTS ? CONVERGENCES ?

By Francis A. Sullivan, S.J.
and Robert Faricy, S.J.

WIPF & STOCK · Eugene, Oregon

Wipf and Stock Publishers
199 W 8th Ave, Suite 3
Eugene, OR 97401

Ignatian Exercises, Charismatic Renewal
Similarities? Differences? Contrasts? Convergences?
By Sullivan, Francis A., SJ and Faricy, Robert, SJ
Copyright©1977 by Sullivan, Francis A., SJ
ISBN 13: 978-61097-474-5
Publication date 4/26/2011
Previously published by Centrum Ignatianum Spiritualitatis, 1977

CONTENTS

INTRODUCTION

This booklet gives the substance of six illuminating talks delivered in Rome by two professors of the Gregorian University. Its chapters point out certain unexpected points of coincidence (and difference) between the Spiritual Exercises of St. Ignatius and the charismatic renewal that is so rapidly growing among Catholics the world over.

The Spiritual Exercises are usually regarded as a closely directed (and even a tightly controlled) process for learning what the Lord's will is for the retreatant, rather than as a means for warm, spontaneous prayer. The Catholic charismatic renewal, on the other hand, is often considered a "fringe practice." But both those judgments are oversimplifications, as the following pages will show.

The authors of this booklet have both been relatively long associated with the Catholic charismatic renewal, and have done considerable teaching and writing about it. Their credentials are impressive.

Father Sullivan has been for 23 years a professor of dogmatic theology at the Gregorian, and in 1971 was one of the first members of Lumen Christi, a Catholic charismatic group in Rome.

Father Farioy, who has been in Rome for 7 years, teaching at the Gregorian's Institute of Spirituality and at the Regina Mundi University, is widely sought after as a lecturer on the charismatic renewal. He too is a member of Lumen Christi.

The Centrum Ignatianum Spiritualitatis (CIS), which sponsored the talks that gave rise to this booklet, hopes that its chapters will help to promote a wider knowledge, not only of the Exercises of St. Ignatius, but also of how the Catholic charismatic renewal fits into the long tradition of the Catholic, and indeed the entire Christian faith.

* * *

THE SPIRITUAL EXERCISES, AND

THE LIFE IN THE SPIRIT SEMINARS

Since almost all of the people following this series of conferences have made a retreat according to the method of St. Ignatius, and only a few have made a Life in the Spirit Seminar, I shall presume an acquaintance with the Spiritual Exercises, so as to have more time to give a detailed explanation of the Life in the Spirit Seminars of the charismatic renewal. For the sake of brevity, I shall speak simply of the "Exercises," the "seminars," and the "renewal," since in the context it will be obvious what each of these terms means.

An experience that changes people's lives

The seminars are built around a spiritual experience that is central to the renewal: an experience that is called the "outpouring of the Spirit" or being "baptized in the Spirit." This will be the subject of my second talk, but since the seminars really cannot be understood except in the light of this experience, I shall have to say something at least briefly about it now.

In my opinion, the remarkable growth of this renewal in the Catholic Church, in the short space of only ten years, can be explained only by the reality of the experience that so many people have had of the changes that took place in their lives, and in the lives of others whom they know, as a result of having been prayed with for a new outpouring of the Spirit, or a new baptism in the Spirit.

Fundamentally, what these people experienced were changes that took place in their lives; to attribute those changes to a release of the Spirit, a new outpouring of the Spirit, or a being baptized in the Spirit is to offer a theological interpretation, to explain the cause of what has happened to one. It is important to understand that the experience comes first, and the interpretation follows later; likewise that differing theological interpretations can be given (e.g., by members of Pentecostal Churches and by Catholics) of what seems to be basically the same kind of experience.

Looking rather at the experience than at varying interpretations of it, there are still reasons to speak of it as "pentecostal," because in many respects it resembles the experience of the first disciples at Pentecost. Jesus promised them that they would "receive power" and would "be his witnesses" through what would happen to them at Pentecost. And we see how they were transformed, from weak, fearful, timid men, to bold, courageous apostles, ready to announce the gospel to the very people who had put Jesus to death.

In our time, many people can testify to something similar happening to them, a new power that has come into their lives, a new strength to live their Christian commitment and to witness to their faith both in word and deed. Like the disciples at Pentecost, very many find themselves moved in a new way to the praise of God, to a sense of the reality of the Lord whom they meet in their prayer, to a totally new realization of what it means that "Jesus is Lord."

The basic experience of the charismatic renewal is that changes like these really take place in a great many people when others have prayed with them for a new outpouring of the Holy Spirit in their lives. In the early days of the renewal in the Catholic Church, people who had had such an experience, in their enthusiasm to share it with others, would pray in this way with practically anyone who requested it, even with someone whom they hardly knew, who had come to join their prayer meeting for the first time.

A preparation is needed for this experience

Among those who began doing this were the young lay leaders of the prayer group in Ann Arbor, Michigan: Ralph Martin and Stephen Clark, the latter of whom describes their experience in the introduction to the Life in the Spirit Team Manual. He tells how they soon came to realize that people needed to be prepared before they were prayed with for the "baptism in the Spirit."

"The Lord was teaching us that we would have to do something more. We would have to introduce people to the life in the Spirit, and not just to the 'baptism in the Spirit.' We would have to teach them how to begin a consistent relationship with Christ in the power of the Spirit. We learned that if we took the emphasis off the spiritual experience of being baptized in the Spirit and put the emphasis on living a new life in the Spirit, people were able to open up to the Lord – and to persevere – more successfully. We also learned that if we took more time and gave more preparation, more would happen with people.

"And so we developed the Life in the Spirit Seminars. While it is certainly true that the Lord can (and frequently does), sovereignly baptize people in the Spirit upon their first contact with the community, the effort given to better preparation leads to more solid fruit in the long run."

9

From this quotation it is clear that the seminars are the fruit of the experience of the leaders of the Ann Arbor group in helping people to reach the best possible dispositions for being prayed with for the baptism in the Spirit. In this respect one can compare them with the Spiritual Exercises, which are the fruit of St. Ignatius's own spiritual experience, as well as of his experience in helping others to seek and find the Lord. In both cases, the books that were written were manuals, intended rather for the use of those helping others, than for the use of those being helped and directed.

We shall now compare the Exercises and the seminars with one another, looking to their respective aims, structures and methods.

The aims of the seminars and the Exercises

It seems to me that the goal at which both the Exercises and the seminars are aiming can be described as a deep and personal conversion to the Lord Jesus Christ. In both cases, such a conversion is seen as a work of God in the soul; it is not something we could accomplish by our own efforts. But at the same time, we have to do as much as we can, with the grace that God gives us, to prepare and dispose ourselves for such a conversion. The Exercises and the seminars are methods that many people have found helpful in reaching such dispositions of soul, but the ultimate aim is the grace for which one wishes to dispose oneself: namely, the deep conversion that only the Lord himself can work in us.

I am not speaking here of a first conversion to the faith, or even, primarily, of a conversion from a life of grave habitual sin, but rather to the kind of conversion of which Karl Rahner is speaking in the following section of his article "Conversion" in *Sacramentum Mundi*:

"Pastoral practice and theology ought not to overlook the phenomenon of conversion as a decisive function of pastoral care of the individual. Not only be-

cause freedom, in the sense of man's unique, historical
self-realization intended to be final in regard to God,
implies a fundamental decision, but also because a decision of this kind ought to be carried out as consciously
and explicitly as possible, since reflection and history
are constitutive of man's very essence. From this point
of view, conversion is not so much or always a turning
away from definite particular sins of the past, as a res-
olute, radical and radically conscious, personal and in
each instance unique adoption of Christian life. And in
this, freedom, decision as absolutely final, and grace
are really experienced (cf. Gal 3:5).

        "Furthermore, in a society which in philosoph-
ical outlook is extremely heterogeneous and anti-Chris-
tian, Christianity in the individual, deprived of support
from the milieu, cannot survive in the long run without
a conversion of this kind, i.e., a personal, fundamental
choice of faith and Christian life. Pastoral theology
and practice should therefore cultivate more the art of
spiritual initiation into this kind of personal experience of conversion... There have been in existence for a
long time in Catholic pastoral practice all kinds of ways
of methodically promoting conversion, adapted to the general human and cultural level of Christians, e.g. popular missions, retreats, days of recollection, novitiates,
etc. All such pastoral methods directed toward conversion ought, however, to be examined to see whether they
are precise enough and correctly adapted to the dispositions of men today to make possible for them a genuine
religious experience and conversion" (Vol. 2,5-6).

        In my opinion, in the Life in the Spirit Sem-
inars we have another such pastoral method, one that seems
particularly well adapted to the dispositions of a great
many people today, and does make possible for them a genuine religious experience and conversion. It hardly
needs to be added that the Spiritual Exercises have proved
themselves, for over four hundred years, to be an effective way of reaching the same goal.

The structure of the seminars and the Exercises

The seminars are usually provided by a prayer group that meets once a week, and hence they follow the rhythm of the prayer meetings, taking place usually either before or after the weekly meeting. An announcement is made during the prayer meeting about a series of seminars to begin within a week or two, and those who wish to take part are invited to sign up in advance or at a preliminary "sign-up meeting." The seminars consist of a series of seven weekly meetings, in each of which a twenty-minute talk is given by one of the leaders, followed by discussion in small groups of three or four participants with a discussion leader. The participants are urged to spend at least fifteen minutes each day during these seven weeks meditating on Scripture texts that bear on the topic presented in each seminar.

As the seminars grew out of the experience of helping people to obtain the greatest possible fruit from the prayer for the baptism in the Spirit, they are structured around the fifth week, when the members of the team pray, with those who request it, for a new outpouring of the Spirit. The first four seminars are designed to help people reach the dispositions of faith and repentance,and the deep desire for conversion to the Lord Jesus Christ, with which they should ask him to pour out his Holy Spirit anew on them. The sixth and seventh seminars are intended to help people to make some practical decisions that will be important to them in their ongoing life in the Spirit, such as the decision to spend some time each day in personal prayer, and to enter fully into the life of a prayer group or community, if they have not already done so.

There is much in the first four seminars that corresponds to the First Week of the Exercises. It is a time for confronting the basic gospel challenge: for recognizing what needs to be changed in my life if I am really going to take the gospel seriously; for repenting of my past sins, for turning to the Lord with a strong desire to be changed and welcoming all the consequences of really accepting Jesus as the Lord of my life.

12

In the fifth seminar the participants are urged to make an act of commitment to Christ, which has much in common with the colloquy that St. Ignatius suggests in his contemplation on the Kingdom of Christ. In this act of commitment, which precedes the prayer for the outpouring of the Spirit, the participants confess their faith in Christ as their Lord, renounce all wrongdoing, and profess their desire to belong wholly to Christ and his Kingdom.

Finally, the emphasis on concrete decisions in the sixth and seventh seminars suggests the primary importance that St. Ignatius puts on the Election to be made during the Second Week of the Exercises.

The method used in the seminars and the Exercises

Most of the differences between the Exercises and the seminars are differences in method. Ideally, the Exercises should be made for a period of thirty days, during which a person withdraws in "retreat," and speaks only to his director. It would be possible to make the seminars in a kind of retreat, but they are ordinarily made, as we have said, by a group of people who meet once a week for the talk and discussion, and spend some time each day in prayer, but otherwise carry on their normal lives.

Whereas the director of an Ignatian retreat is usually a priest or religious who has been trained for this ministry, the team directing the seminars is made up of members of the prayer group that sponsors the seminars. Sometimes there will be a priest or religious on the team, but very often, for the lack of such people in the prayer group, the team will be composed entirely of lay people, none of whom has professional training in spiritual direction.

Experience has shown that such people can lead others in these seminars effectively, because it is very much a question of communicating a spiritual experience that they have personally had themselves. For this reason, in the talks and discussions, a primary emphasis is put on the leaders' personal witness to their own experience of turning to the Lord and receiving the gift of his Spirit in a new way. This witness is all the more effective precisely because it is coming, not from professionally religious people, but from laymen and laywomen with whom the participants in the seminar can easily identify.

Finally, what surely must be seen as the key point in which the seminars differ from the Spiritual Exercises, is the primary importance they give to the explicit prayer made by the group leaders for each participant who requests it, for a new outpouring of the Spirit. As we have seen, the seminars are structured around this prayer, to help people to prepare for it and to obtain the most fruit from it. On the surface, at least, there is nothing in the Spiritual Exercises that corresponds to this. In our next talk we shall look under the surface, to see whether anything in the Exercises corresponds to what people in the charismatic renewal call "being baptized in the Spirit."

* * *

14

THE FIRST WEEK OF THE EXERCISES, AND
THE PRAYER FOR INNER HEALING

The Spiritual Exercises of Ignatius Loyola are far more than simply a way to make a retreat. They form the basis for a way of life shared not only by the members of the religious order Ignatius founded but by thousands of other persons. The Exercises make up a structure of consciousness. So, too, the contemporary charismatic renewal goes far beyond just a way some people pray together at meetings. It too strikes deeper, can be a whole way of life, forming personal prayer as well as common prayer, and influences every aspect of life; like the Exercises, it is fundamentally a structure of consciousness.

In other words, both phrases - Spiritual Exercises and charismatic renewal - describe spiritualities. What do these two spiritualities have to say to one another? How do they overlap, compare, differ, and possibly contribute to each other?

The First Week and Prayer for inner healing

Here I want to take up two at least apparently similar elements of the Exercises and the renewal: the First Week of the Spiritual Exercises, and the practice of praying for inner healing in the charismatic renewal.

Both involve, in different ways, an encounter with the Lord in terms of the disorder in one's life; they have, for content, the same reality of a sinful, hurt, disordered person before the loving and merciful Lord. The First Week, like prayer for inner healing, has to do with areas of personal identity, with self-understanding, with the identity that emerges from one's personal history, with who one is, as a person, in relationship with others and particularly in relationship with God. Prayer for inner healing focuses on the healing of wounds and hurts in a person's past; the First Week concentrates rather on sorrow for one's sinfulness. Nevertheless, they have in common that they include, somehow, an awareness of being held captive in a hurtful and sinful frame of reference. They both minister to the effects of sin in the person, the effects of inherited (original) sin and the effects of personal sins.

Again, both the First Week and prayer for inner healing look to an experience of the Lord. Moreover, they have in common that they both center, not on the *experience* of the Lord, but on the *Lord* of the experience. They stress the unmerited love of God for the person, and they underline God's initiative in the love relationship between himself and the person.

It could be thought that the First Week of the Exercises looks to the initiative of the retreatant rather than to the divine initiative, but even a superficial examination of the text is enough to dispel that false conception. In all the meditations of the First Week, after a first prelude, which situates the retreatant with regard to the meditation's content, the second prelude is "to ask of God our Lord that which I wish and desire: shame and lowliness at one's sins" (First Exercise), or "great and intense grief, and tears for my sins" (Second Exercise). The Third Exercise repeats the first two and adds prayers for three graces: "first, that I may feel an interior knowledge of my sins and a detestation of them; second, that I may feel the disorder of my actions in order that, abhorring that disorder, I may reform and lead an ordered life; third, to ask for a knowledge of the world so that, abhorring it, I may put away from myself worldly and vain things." It is grace that is prayed for; the power is expected to come from God, not from the retreatant. This prayer for grace, for the power of the Lord to give the retreatant interior and *felt* knowledge of the disorder in himself and in the world, is repeated in the Fourth Exercise.

The additions and notes of the First Week make several suggestions that could help the retreatant in this first phase of the Spiritual Exercises. All of these are directed to a psychological disposition suitable for the reception of the graces of the First Week, the graces prayed for in the second preludes of each of the exercises. But Ignatius makes it clear that what is sought is grace, that the initiative and the power are the Lord's.

The First Week and the Second Seminar

The content of the First Week parallels to some extent the material of the second seminar of the Life in the Spirit Seminars Team Manual. This manual, widely used, translated into several languages, gives the philosophy, procedure and outlines for the seven one-hour seminars that make up the standard initiation into the charismatic renewal. During the fifth seminar, those following the program are prayed with for the reception of the outpouring of the Spirit, or as it is commonly called,

the baptism in the Spirit. The first four seminars lead up to the fifth.

The first, on God's love, serves the same purpose as the First Principle and Foundation of the Spiritual Exercises: to orient the participant toward God in an open and expectant way. And, it seems to me, the second seminar, on salvation, has somewhat the same purpose as Ignatius Loyola's First Week: to point out and to help the participants *feel* the need for salvation, the need for the Lord. The main points of these seminar talks, as given in the Team Manual, are: 1) "There is something seriously wrong with the world, with society as a whole and with individual lives. Something major is needed." 2) "Since the cause of what is wrong with society is bigger than men can handle on their own (Satan, sin, and the dominion of darkness), men need God to find the new life they want." 3) "God sent Jesus, his Son, to break the hold of Satan and give us new life through his death and resurrection. Jesus is the Lord and Savior." The point, of course, is to bring the person making the seminars into an awareness of his sinfulness and of his existence in a sinful world, an awareness of his need for Jesus as Savior. For the world, and the participant in the seminar, need redemption – and the redeemer has to be Jesus.

In some charismatic groups, a prayer for inner healing takes place in either the third or the fourth seminar session: after the second seminar, which brings the person to recognize the disorder in himself or herself, and before the prayer in the fifth seminar for the outpouring of the Spirit. A French-language adaptation of the Team Manual (*Afin que vous portiez beaucoup de fruits*, Père Philippe, O.S.B., Maison de Prière "La Vigne"; Brussels, 1974) contains considerable material in its third seminar talk explaining inner healing, and devotes the fourth seminar to a group prayer for the inner healing of the participants. There are two good reasons for such a prayer: first, a person has to become aware of his inner disorder before he can act to correct it; and second, he may be so blocked by his disorder tnat he cannot really receive the effects of the baptism in the Spirit. An in-between step may be needed at this point:

18

a prayer for interior healing once the person is concious of his need for such healing, so as to bring his inner life back into harmony again and let the effects of the outpouring or baptism of the Spirit become manifest.

Ordinarily, however, prayer for inner healing does not take place in a large group, but rather on a one-to-one basis, or with perhaps two people praying for the inner healing of a third. A confessor can pray for inner healing for a penitent during or immediately after the sacrament of penance. One can simply pray oneself for one's own inner healing - and this is the most common.

Prayer for inner healing: what is it?

All of us, at least sometimes, have experienced inner suffering, or conflicts, or strong and unreasonable anger or fear or sadness. We know from the gospels that Jesus can heal us, not only physically, but also interiorly, psychologically, emotionally, spiritually. We know, too, that prayers are answered.

Often our Lord will work through some people to heal others, for example, through psychological counseling. However, Jesus also heals simply in answer to prayer for inner healing. This means that we can pray for and with others that they be healed in their emotions, and it means that we ourselves can pray to be healed interiorly.

We know from psychology and psychiatry that much of what needs to be healed in us is buried beneath the level of consciousness. Interior suffering or stress or sadness frequently results from root problems or hurts or wounds or conflicts that are not conscious, that we are not aware of. We see only the tips of the icebergs that need to be melted. It's not necessary to know with precision what needs healing, although it helps. We can pray to be healed, interiorly, in our emotions, insofar as we are aware that we need healing, and then we can let the Lord take it from there and guide us to what we should do or pray for next.

Where do these (usually unconscious) hurts come from? They come from the very beginning of our existence, from our earliest years, from our childhood and growing up, from the whole process of living. Some of them are so early and so deeply repressed that we can never get at them; but our Lord sees them all and can heal them all. Many interior wounds, whether conscious or buried, result from poor or inadequate home life in childhood, from negative aspects of school life, from setbacks in childhood or later life. In many cases, things have been done to people that ought never to have been done, a lot of suffering was caused, and healing is needed.

What are the conditions for inner healing? They are two: 1) aith, that we believe in Jesus's power to heal us per· jnally; and 2) forgiveness of others.

ᴊod acts in and through Jesus. And he asks us to believe not only in his love but also in his power, for his love is powerful and it heals. Believing in Jesus's love for me is one thing. But more is needed: belief in the force of his love, in the healing power of his compassion for me personally. The healing power of the humanity of Jesus is surely not less than it was when he helped people during his public ministry; if anything, it is greater after his resurrection. And he has promised us that he hears and answers our prayers.

Inner healing and forgiveness

The second condition of inner healing is that I forgive others. Failure to forgive other persons the pain and the hurt that they have caused me can block me, can close me to the healing power of Jesus. The resentment or the anger that I feel toward a person who has hurt me can· act as a hard shell around the inner wound that that person caused. That hard casing of resentment or bitterness can screen the hurt from Jesus's healing power.

Failure to forgive other persons the pain and the hurt that they have caused can block me, can close me to the healing power of Jesus. Inner healing of the emotions depends to a great extent on reconciliation with God. It depends on repentance for sins and God's consequent forgiveness of those sins. Repentance and acceptance of God's mercy in reconciliation with him is a kind of inner healing, a spiritual healing. And it is closely connected with emotional healing and can often lead to it. On the other hand, little healing of the emotions by the power of the Holy Spirit is possible unless repentance and reconciliation with God are present.

However, the grace of repentance frequently depends on my forgiving others. God can forgive us only insofar as we forgive others; and so we pray "forgive us our trespasses as we forgive those who trespass against us"; "forgive us our sins as we forgive those who sin against us." If I do not forgive others, the hurt or bitterness or resentment or anger inside me keeps me from that repentance and openness to God that are necessary for my acceptance of God's forgiveness — and so for the healing of my emotions and feelings.

Sometimes our failure to forgive is buried, lies below the level of awareness. We think, or we take for granted, that we have forgiven others; but our resentment and unforgiveness remain inside us, not conscious. This is why it is often important to forgive those who have hurt us, whether they intended to or not, even when we are not aware of any bitterness or lack of forgiveness on our part.

And many of us need to forgive ourselves for our sins, our mistakes, and our failures. I need to accept Jesus's and the Father's total and unconditional acceptance of me; accepting God's acceptance of me, I can accept myself. Our Lord loves me, not in spite of the dark side of myself, but partly because of it; he came to save not the just, but sinners; and my sinfulness attracts his loving compassion. Accepting his compassionate and loving forgiveness and acceptance of me, I can forgive myself.

Sometimes we need to forgive God. Obviously, there is no fault at all in God. Nevertheless, I may feel, in a vague way, some resentment against God for my own limitations or failures, for illness or an accident, for the death of someone I love, or for circumstances of my

life. God wants me to forgive him, so that I can get over
my resentment, accept his love better, and be healed.

Inner healing can take place in personal prayer
when a person prays alone. It can take place in a group
where inner healing is prayed for. The privileged situations for healing to take place are the sacraments, especially confession of sins, the anointing of the sick,
and the Eucharist celebration of the Lord's Supper.

When I confess my sins, I can express sorrow for
them, receive God's pardon and his peace – and also pray
for and receive healing of the wounds and hurts that may
be connected with the sins I confessed or that may be at
the root of the sinful tendencies that resulted in those
sins. The sacrament of the anointing of the sick is not
only in preparation for the life to come, but for forgiveness of sins and for both bodily and inner healing. The
Eucharist, especially, is the sacrament of the healing of
personal relationships, of being made more one in Jesus
through sharing "the same bread." And, in general, the
prayer "... but only say the word and I shall be healed"
is meant to be said in faith, with a faith that is hope-
ful, that *expects* (for hope is expectation in faith)
healing to take place.

Inner healing and conversion

So far I have considered inner healing somewhat
as an isolated action, a result of an explicit prayer for
healing. Inner healing can also be situated within the
total process of encountering the Lord; seen this way,
inner healing can be understood more realistically. Furthermore, it can be understood better as an integral part
of growth in union with the Lord, as a condition of deep
conversion, and as leading to service. And its relationship with the First Week will be evident.

The story of the meeting between Jesus and the
Samaritan woman (Jn 4:7-42) casts light on the place of
inner healing as part of the process of prayer. The process begins with a journey, a movement toward the Lord,

22

ending with a stopping short in his presence. There takes place a bringing into awareness of the disorder in the woman's life and the beginning of a reordering. This incipient reordering itself initiates a conversion process that clarifies the woman's understanding of herself - as a sinner and as called. In turn, conversion brings her closer to the Lord and gives her a new freedom, which takes shape in mission: she goes out to the other Samaritans with the good news, having accepted a call that names her personally and that goes beyond that to become a call to go to others, a sending to bring the good news of the Lord.

The healing of Peter's mother-in-law (Mk 1:29-31) shows the same connection between healing and service. "The fever left her, and she served them." The received healing becomes a new freedom to serve. It occurs commonly, when a person receives a healing from the Lord, that the person looks for some form of service to give shape to his gratitude and his freedom.

I have been describing the relationships between the First Week and the contemplation on the Kingdom. The First Week is a prolonged prayerful encounter with the Lord in the framework of the retreatant's own sinfulness and disorder of self and of life, and, balancing that disorder, the Lord's merciful love. This is an inner healing situation. And the healing that takes place leads right into the contemplation on the call of the King - so much so that the Kingdom contemplation is as much a part of the First Week as it is of the Second. (This may be why Ignatius sets it apart as not properly belonging to either week).

It seems to me that, in some cases, perhaps many, prayer for inner healing would be appropriate during the course of the Spiritual Exercises, particularly at the end of the First Week, or perhaps in the context of the confession that is normally made during the First Week, and before the contemplation on the Kingdom. Just as prayer for inner healing is often called for before the effects of the baptism in the Spirit are felt, so too perhaps we should pray for inner healing before the contemplation on the Kingdom, and those of the Second Week too, to be sure they will have their full impact. Like the baptism in the Spirit, the Kingdom contemplation is intended to be the high point of a conversion experience. Often, interior healing needs to happen before an interior conversion can really take root and be a substantial and permanent change.

Prayer. Perhaps, right now, we can pray, combining the First Week and prayer for inner healing, making a kind of mini-First Week plus prayer for inner healing. We can ask for the over-all grace of the second preludes of the First Week. Then we can, with the Lord's help, forgive those who have hurt us. And then we can ask him to heal us.

"Lord Jesus Christ, I ask you for the grace to help me to be aware of the disorder in my inner self, to help me to see and experience my own interior disorder, and hurts and wounds, and sinfulness."

Perhaps right now each of you can bring to mind some interior pain, some inner wound. It may be a failure or a broken friendship or the loss of a person you love. It can be something in childhood, such as a poor relationship with your mother or your father. It can be a present sense of failure, or depression, or anger toward someone, or a feeling of coldness toward a person we used to love. So then: right now, before Jesus, forgive anyone who may have caused such a hurt. Tell Jesus that you forgive them. And, right now, ask Jesus for the healing of your hurt feelings and emotions. Pray with me:

"Jesus, you have promised us that if we ask we shall receive, and that if we knock it will be opened to us. I claim your promise. I come to you like a little child and I ask you in faith to heal me. I forgive everyone who has hurt me. And I present this inner hurt to the healing power of your Holy Spirit. Heal me, Jesus. Take away the pain. And fill the healed place with your love. Amen."

* * *

THE 'EXPERIENCE' OF THE EXERCISES, AND
THE PENTECOSTAL BAPTISM IN THE SPIRIT

We have seen that both the Spiritual Exercises and the charismatic renewal aim at a deep personal conversion to Jesus as Lord, and both try to lead people to such a conversion by confronting them with the basic message of the gospel. Every genuine renewal in the history of Christianity has involved a new hearing of the gospel and a new, more radical response to its challenge. In every case this has meant a new way of responding to the person of Jesus Christ.

Given the richness of his person, and of his message, the various great renewals in history have been able to stress one or other facet of what it means to take the gospel seriously. Thus it has been possible to bring out of the treasure "both what is new and what is old" (Mt 13:52). The Franciscan revival, for example, was sparked by a new hearing and response to Jesus's teaching and example of poverty and simplicity. Ignatian spirituality is marked in a special way by a desire to follow Christ not only in poverty but also in opprobrium and humiliation.

Jesus pours out his Spirit on us

I think one can express what is distinctive about the way the basic gospel message is presented in the charismatic renewal by saying that it wishes to communicate the *whole* of the Good News that Peter announced for the first time at Pentecost: not only that Jesus died to save sinners, but that he is Lord, that he has poured out the Spirit, and that he will give the same Spirit to all who repent of their sins and accept him as their Lord (Ac 2:22-42).

Substantially, this is the message of the first five weeks of the Life in the Spirit Seminars. "It was you who crucified Jesus by your sins; but God does not hold this against you. He has raised Jesus from the dead as your Savior; by believing in him you can save yourselves from this crooked generation. Jesus is now the Lord, at the right hand of the Father; the proof of this is that it is he who now pours out the Holy Spirit on all who accept him as their Lord. Believe in him, then, repent of your former way of life, accept him with all your heart as your Lord, and you will receive from him this promised gift of the Holy Spirit."

In addition, one can see the message of the last two seminars in the description that Luke gives us of the first Christian community: "So those who received his word were baptized, and there were added that day about three thousand souls. And they devoted themselves to the apostles' teaching, and fellowship, to the breaking of bread and the prayers" (Ac 2:41-42). We have seen how the talks in the sixth and seventh seminars stress the importance of a decision to enter fully into the life of a prayer group or community, if one has not already done so.

If it is true, as I believe it is, that the message of the charismatic renewal is essentially the Good News announced by Peter on the first Pentecost, in all its fullness, then the crucial question has to do with the application to already baptized Christians, of Ac 2: 38: "Repent and be baptized every one of you in the name of Jesus Christ for the forgiveness of your sins, and you shall receive the gift of the Holy Spirit."

At this point I would like to recall something I said early in my first talk: namely, that in the charismatic renewal, as indeed in the New Testament itself, experience comes first, and theological interpretation of the experience follows afterward. What people in the charismatic renewal have experienced is that when baptized Christians respond to this message in a new, personal way, and accepting Jesus as Lord of their lives, with all that this will mean by way of changing their former way of living, and asking other Christians to pray with them for a new gift of the Holy Spirit, real changes very often do take place which strongly suggest that the Holy Spirit is indeed at work in them in a new, more evident, and more powerful way.

A new 'baptism' for baptized Christians

I believe that such experiences, which are now both widespread and well attested, justify us in concluding that there is in fact a sense in which the promise of Ac 2:38 applies also to already baptized Christians. Obviously, they cannot receive the sacrament of baptism again. But "to be baptized in the name of Jesus Christ" involves the personal will to be consecrated to him, to accept him as one's personal Lord and Savior.

It is quite possible that a Christian who was baptized as an infant, never really made his own what was done for him by others at his christening. It is quite possible that the sacrament of confirmation did not have such a meaning for him either. In such a case, which surely is not so uncommon, I think one is correct in saying

that a person's Christian initiation still needs to be completed. Even though it is complete *sacramentally*, as far as what is done to a person is concerned, there is still something lacking in regard to the person's *appropriation* of what was done to him.

Furthermore, I believe that one can rightly speak of various levels or degrees of personal appropriation of sacramental initiation. There can be a great difference, for instance, between the depth of personal decision involved in an adolescent reception of confirmation, and the kind of profound conversion that one can find either in the Spiritual Exercises or in the charismatic renewal.

Basically, the message of the charismatic renewal is that the promise of Ac 2:38 has a meaning also for baptized Christians. This message is not mere theory, but the fruit of experience: namely, that when Christians hear the gospel anew and wish to accept Jesus as their Lord in a more radical way, they should ask other Christians to pray with them for a new outpouring of the Spirit in their lives, and this prayer will be answered.

Of course, they are not receiving the Holy Spirit for the first time. But if this is the first time someone has made a really personal decision to live as a Christian, I think we may speak of it as the completion of his Christian initiation. If he has made such a decision before, but is now making it at a deeper, more total level, it still seems reasonable to think that prayer made with such dispositions for a new outpouring of the Spirit will be answered. In any case, the experience of people in the charismatic renewal is that very frequently, after such prayer, changes do take place in the lives of Christians, which strongly suggest that the Holy Spirit is at work in them in a new way.

But one might ask: even granted that genuine conversions do take place in answer to such prayer as this, even granted that people really are changed, is it in accordance with our Catholic tradition to attribute such effects as these to a new outpouring of the Spirit? Is not the Holy Spirit given at baptism? Can we speak of any subsequent, non-sacramental experience as a person's "baptism in the Holy Spirit"?

28

'Baptism' in a metaphorical sense

The first thing to keep in mind is that in
the phrase "baptize in the Holy Spirit," the word "baptize" is being used in a metaphorical sense. Nowadays,
we hardly ever use this word except of the sacrament of
Christian initiation. But in New Testament times the
word "baptize" was still being used with its original
meaning: "to plunge, immerse, drench," and in various
metaphorical meanings derived from this.

Thus, for instance, when Jesus spoke of "the
baptism with which he was to be baptized" (Mk 10:38-39),
he was describing his future passion as like a torrent or
flood that would overwhelm him. So also, when John the
Baptist prophesied that Jesus was to "baptize in the Holy
Spirit and fire" (Lk 3:16; Mt 3:11), he was using the
word in a figurative sense, in contrast to the literal
sense in which he himself was baptizing in water. In
Acts, Luke sees the fulfillment of John's prophecy in
the outpouring of the Spirit on the disciples at Pentecost, and later, on Cornelius and his household (Ac 1:5
and 11:16). To "pour out the Spirit" is of course another
biblical metaphor, used in both Old and New Testaments,
which, like "baptize in the Spirit," is based on the image
of the Spirit as "living water."

Personally, I prefer to speak of a "new outpouring of the Spirit," rather than of "baptism in the
Spirit," because of the misunderstandings to which the
latter term can easily give rise in the minds of people
who are accustomed to think of baptism only in connection
with the sacrament.

To return to the question previously raised,
then: is it in accordance with our Catholic tradition to
attribute such effects as we see taking place in people in
the charismatic renewal, to a "new outpouring of the
Spirit?" If a person has already been baptized and con-
firmed, and is living in the state of grace, can we expect that he could still receive a new outpouring of the
Spirit in answer to prayer?

It is true that some Catholic theologians in
this renewal prefer to speak of the Holy Spirit as "poured

out" or "given" in the sacraments, and to explain what is
called "baptism in the Spirit" as a "release" or a "coming into conscious experience" of the gift of the Spirit
already received in Christian initiation. I have no
objections to such an explanation, provided one does not
imply that there is something inconsistent with Catholic
theology in the idea of a new sending or new outpouring
of the Spirit that can take place after a Christian has
received the sacraments of baptism and confirmation.

For it is the clear teaching of St. Thomas
that there can be new "sendings" of the Spirit to a person
in whom the Spirit is already indwelling by grace. He
sees evidence of a new sending of the Spirit whenever a
decisive change has taken place in a person's life that
can be described as a "moving forward into a new act or
new state of grace." As examples of such "new acts or
states of grace," he mentions receiving the grace of
working miracles, of prophesying, offering one's life as
a martyr, renouncing all one's possessions, etc. (*Summa
Th*. I, q.43, a.6, ad 2). His argument is this: where
changes like this take place, one can say that the Holy
Spirit is doing something new in this person. Where the
Holy Spirit is doing something decisively new, one can
say that he is present in a new way. And when the Holy
Spirit begins to be present in a new say, working a real
innovation in this person's life, we can speak of a "new
sending" or "new outpouring" of the Spirit.

It is my conviction that in many cases the
changes that take place in people in the charismatic
renewal can be described as a "move into a new state of
grace" such as St. Thomas does not hesitate to attribute
to a new sending of the Holy Spirit. I believe that I
am on safe theological ground when I say that what people
are praying for, and many are receiving, is truly a new
outpouring of the Holy Spirit.

Is there an 'outpouring' in the Exercises?

Is there anything that corresponds to this in
the Spiritual Exercises? Of course, there is nothing like

the practice of having a group of people gather around a person to pray explicitly that he or she may receive a new outpouring of the Spirit. But if we ask what St. Ignatius expected to happen to the "devout soul" in the course of the Exercises, we shall find something remarkably similar, in substance of not in language, to what is sought in the renewal.

St. Ignatius tells us what he expects to happen in the course of the Exercises, in his 15th Annotation: "The director of the Exercises ought not to urge the exercitant more to poverty or any promise than to the contrary, nor to one state of life or way of living more than to another. Outside the Exercises, it is true, we may lawfully and meritoriously urge all who probably have the required fitness to choose continence, virginity, the religious life, and every form of religious perfection. But while one is engaged in the Spiritual Exercises, it is more suitable and much better that the Creator and Lord in person communicate himself to the devout soul in quest of the divine will, that he inflame it with his love and praise, and dispose it for the way in which it could better serve God in the future. Therefore, the director of the Exercises, like a balance at equilibrium, without leaning to one side or the other, should let the Creator deal directly with the creature, and the creature directly with his Creator and Lord."

Here we see that what St. Ignatius expects to happen to a person making the Exercises is nothing less than that God will communicate himself to this soul. This is no created gift of grace, but the uncreated Gift of God himself. But is it not the Holy Spirit who is most properly named *Donum*, the "Gift?" And if we accept this translation (there is some uncertainty about the original Spanish at this point), what more perfectly reflects the work of the Holy Spirit in a soul than to "*inflame* it with the love and praise" of its Creator?

Indeed, when we read a passage like this in the Exercises, we can only ask why St. Ignatius does not speak explicitly of the Holy Spirit as the uncreated gift by which God communicates himself to the soul. Very likely his reticence about the Holy Spirit in the book of the Exercises is to be explained by his care not to say

anything that could arouse suspicion of Illuminism. But
there is no reason *now* why we should not recognize the
Holy Spirit in those passages of the Exercises in which
St. Ignatius speaks of "the Creator and Lord communicating
himself to the soul, inflaming it with his love and praise,"
or where he says (in the Rules for the Discernment of
Spirits) that "it belongs solely to the Creator to come
into a soul, to leave it, to act upon it, to draw it wholly to the love of his Divine Majesty."

          In support of this view, I would like to quote
what Fathers Maurizio Flick and Zoltan Alszeghy, professors of theology at the Gregorian University, say in the
little book (*Il Mese di Esercizi, L'Esperienza di Galloro,*
Stella Matutina, Roma, 1972, 52-55) that is the fruit of
their long experience of directing priests and seminari-
ans in 30-day retreats. Here is their comment on the 15th
Annotation:

          "Basically, the experience that is character-
istic of the Exercises is a self-communication of God to
man... Such an event is a psychological process which,
in the light of faith, reveals itself as a work of grace...
The Exercises, from a theological point of view, are simply
an effort, made under the influence of grace, to cooperate
with grace, to dispose oneself to receive grace, to follow
faithfully the impulses of grace. A person who lives this
experience nowadays will be inclined to express this in
language that is more personalistic and for that very
reason more biblical: he will say that in the Exercises
one opens oneself to the Spirit, who works the interior
transformation of man. The Divine Master assures us that
the Father will not refuse the good Spirit to those who ask
it (Lk 11:13). If perservering in the month of the Exercises is nothing else than a knocking, a seeking, an asking
for this Spirit, it is impossible that this hope should be
disappointed."

                              * * *

32

THE CONTEMPLATION ON THE KINGDOM, AND

THE LORDSHIP OF JESUS

In the gospels of Matthew, Mark and Luke, the Kingdom occupies a central place in the teaching of Jesus, it is one of his main themes. In the Acts of the Apostles, and especially in the Pauline writings, the theme of the Kingdom becomes the theme of the lordship of Jesus. I would like to describe the New Testament concept of Jesus's lordship, then to comment on how this concept works out in action in the contemporary charismatic renewal, and finally to say something about the contemplation on the Kingdom in the Spiritual Exercises.

The lordship of Jesus in the Gospels and the Acts

The key to the whole idea of Jesus's lordship is his use of Psalm 110. This stands behind the early Church's understanding that Jesus is Lord, and, surely, is at the very origin of the concept. The title "Lord" is applied to Jesus rarely by the synoptic writers, with the exception of Luke, who uses it 18 times. Jesus does not apply the title to himself during his public ministry, and - as the Acts and the Pauline writings show clearly - the primitive Christian community understood Jesus to be constituted Lord by his passion, death and resurrection.

It is, then, to Jesus's use of Psalm 110 that one must look. The context is one of public exchange with the Pharisees (Mt 22:41-46) and the scribes (Mk 12:35-37; Lk 20:41-44). "And as Jesus taught in the temple, he said 'How can the scribes say that the Christ is the son of David? David himself, inspired by the Holy Spirit declared, "The Lord said to my Lord, sit at my right hand till I put thy enemies under thy feet." David himself calls him Lord, so how is he his son?' And the great throng heard him gladly" (Mk 12:35-37).

Psalm 110 is referred to again in the synoptic gospels in conjunction with a reference to the messianic passage Daniel 7, 14 (Mt 26:64; Mk 14:61; Lk 22:69), when the high priest confronts Jesus. "Again the high priest asked him, 'Are you the Christ, the Son of the Blessed?' And Jesus said, 'I am; and you will see the Son of Man seated at the right hand of power, and coming with the clouds of heaven'" (Mk 14:60-61).

Jesus identifies himself with Daniel 7:14's Son of Man figure who comes with the clouds of heaven. But the phrase "seated at the right hand of power" is from Psalm 110: "sit at my right hand." Here, having already entered into the paschal mystery, in his passion, Jesus identifies himself, by his use of Psalm 110, with the "Lord" to whom the Lord speaks in verse 1. The whole passion story itself, with a kind of sublime and mysterious irony that one can hardly grasp, speaks of Jesus as King and Lord particularly in the passages concerning his being mocked, his conversation with Pilate, his presentation by Pilate to the people ("ecce homo") and the inscription on the cross ("King of the Jews").

How did the learned people of Jesus's time understand Psalm 110? Something can be gleaned from the Talmud and from the Midrash on Psalm 110; even though these were compiled much later, they reflect opinions handed down from earlier periods. There is nothing in the Jerusalem Talmud, but the more important Babylonian Talmud contains two significant mentions of Psalm 110, identifying the (second) "lord" with Abraham. However, the Midrash on Psalm 110, also equating Abraham and the "lord," points out that verse 1 of Psalm 110 is at the same time a messianic text. At any rate, Jesus's messianic use of the text tells us that it was considered, at least by some at that time, to be messianic. We can only speculate on Jesus's own study of Psalm 110 as "he grew in age and grace and wisdom," and of his use of it in his explanation of the Scriptures to the two disciples on the road to Emmaus.

The early Church's use of the title "Lord" for Jesus refers to the risen and glorified Jesus, with a certain emphasis on his divinity (he is at the right hand of the Father). The word "lord," *kyrios,* is the word for God in the Septuagint Greek of the Old Testament; in most English translations of the Old Testament it is rendered as "Lord" (although the Jerusalem Bible uses "Yahweh"). Using the same title for Jesus, of course, is to say he is equal to God the Father.

Psalm 110, already part of the basic kerygma of the Church in its first beginnings, is also used in the Pentecost discourse of Peter (Ac 2:34-36), who concludes, "Let all the house of Israel therefore know assuredly that God has made him both Lord and Christ, this Jesus whom you crucified." Stephen, at his death by stoning, gazes upward and sees "the Son of Man standing at the right hand of God" (Ac 7:56). And further, some evidence shows that the mysterious "baptism in the name of Jesus" refers to the liturgical practice that had the person baptized say, during the rite, "Jesus is Lord."

The lordship of Jesus in the Pauline writings

In any case, the phrase "Jesus is Lord" is one of the oldest in the Pauline writings. It occurs six times (Ph 2:11; 1 Co 8:6 and 12:3; 2 Co 4:5; Rm 10:9;

Col 2:6), and certainly antedates all the letters. Add to
this the phrase *marana tha*("Come, Lord") or *maran atha*
("the Lord is coming") of 1 Co 16:22, a phrase that is
repeated in the Apocalypse (22:20b).

Perhaps most interesting is the much commented
on passage of Ph 2:5-11: "Have this mind among yourselves
which is yours in Christ Jesus, who though he was in the
form of God, did not count equality with God a thing to be
grasped, but emptied himself, taking the form of a servant,
being born in the likeness of men. And being formed in
human form, he humbled himself and became obedient unto
death, even death on a cross. Therefore, God has highly
exalted him and bestowed on him the name which is above
every name, that at the same of Jesus every knee should
bow, in heaven and on earth, and every tongue confess that
Jesus Christ is Lord, to the glory of God the Father."

The "name which is above every name" is the
title "Lord," given to Jesus as the divine response to his
suffering and death, to his "emptying out" of himself, his
kenosis, which begins with his incarnation and reaches a
high (or rather, low) point in his death on a cross. The
contrast between "the form of God" (*morphe theou*) and
"human form" (*morphe doulou*) is meant to be striking. The
stress is on Jesus's humility and obedience ("even unto
death") to the Father. In the final point of his *kenosis*,
his death, Jesus descends into the heart of the world so
that, in his resurrection, he can be the heart of the
world, Lord in a true and even ontological way, not simply
appointed or named juridically, but Lord in such a way
that to uproot him would be to make the world cease to
exist.

The same doctrine of Jesus's universal and
organic (as opposed to merely juridical) lordship is
contained in the first three chapters of the Letters to
the Ephesians. "He (the Father) has put all things under
his (Jesus's) feet, and made him, as the ruler of everything, the head of the Church, which is his body, and the
fullness of him who fills the whole creation" (Ep 1:22).
"All things under his feet," as well as the strongly im-
plicit idea of lordship, has echoes of Psalm 110.

The letter to the Colossians (1:13 to 2:15),
and especially what appears to be a previously existing

hymn (1:15-20), views the whole universe as somehow sus-
pended from Christ, anchored in him: "in him all things
hold together" (verse 17) and "for in him all the fullness
of God was pleased to dwell, and through him to reconcile
to himself all things" (verses 19-20). The image differs
from that of the Letter to the Ephesians, where Christ is
seen as filling the universe. Here, in the Letter to the
Colossians, the image is the opposite - of all things being
(reconciled to God) in Christ - but the doctrine is the
same: the universal lordship of Jesus.

Because all creation comes under Jesus's
lordship, all of creation shares in God's plan of salvation. "Creation still retains the hope of being freed,
like us, from its slavery to decadence, to enjoy the same
freedom and glory as the children of God. From the beginning till now the entire creation, as we know, has been
groaning in one great act of giving birth" (Rm 8:21-22).
The world is related to Christ through people in such a
way that the world itself is an object of salvation, of
redemption, of final transformation. Jesus, through us,
is the hope of the world and the guarantee to us of the
meaningfulness of the world. He is the Father's promise
that something permanent will endure, out of what we
make, suffer, and work through in the world.

The Letter to the Hebrews (1:13) quotes Psalm
110 at the end of a series of "proof texts" to show the
lordship of Jesus (see also 8:1, and 10:12-13). And it
goes further than the other Pauline writings in its use
of Psalm 110, taking up the idea of the priesthood according to Melchisedek (Psalm 110, verse 4: Hebrews 6:20
to 7:21), thus associating Jesus's priesthood with his
lordship.

The lordship of Jesus in the charismatic renewal

"Jesus is Lord" is almost the slogan of the
contemporary charismatic renewal. It is said, repeated,
shouted, and sung. What does it mean in practice? What
is the insight of the charismatic renewal into the
meaning of Jesus's lordship for the everyday life of the
Christian?

37

Besides recognizing Jesus's lordship over everything, we are called to recognize Jesus as our own personal Lord. Just as the Lord Jesus gives meaning and existence to the whole world, so he gives me my personal meaning and existence. Just as all history finds its true meaning and fulfillment in Jesus, so I find my own true meaning and fulfillment in him. Jesus risen is present in all of history and in the whole universe, and he is actively present in my whole personal history and in every part of my life. I find my personal value, meaning, existence, and fulfillment in the risen Jesus. And just as the Father's plan from the beginning of time has been to recapitulate all things in Christ, to unify and reconcile everything in Jesus; so, too, the Father's plan is and always has been to unify and to reconcile in Jesus everything in my being and in my life, to integrate me, to give me personal unity, to knit up the frazzled parts of myself, in and through and under the lordship of Jesus.

Jesus calls me not only to accept his love and his lordship, but to actively participate in the Father's plan to recapitulate all things in himself. Jesus invites me to bring everything in my life under his lordship: my worries, my problems, my anxieties and fears, my failures, my successes, my hopes for myself and for others, every-thing. I can take each preoccupation, every burden, all difficulties and sorrows and joys to Jesus, placing them in his hands, under his loving lordship.

To the extent that I do, I will be co-operating with Jesus in his becoming the Lord of my whole life in a conscious way on my part. My prayer and my other activi-ties will become more and more integrated so that my whole life becomes a prayer. My life will cease to be torn in two directions between an "upward" component of faith in God, of worship and love of God, and a "forward" component of faith in other persons, in my work, in the whole human enterprise in general and in my particular part in that enterprise. I will stop being torn between the "vertical" and the "horizontal." The Lord will make an integration in me, a synthesis of all the elements and aspects of my life; he does this with my co-operation, as I bring every-thing in my life, consciously and explicitly, prayerfully, under his lordship.

When people in charismatic renewal say that "Jesus is Lord," this is what they are talking about. They are celebrating his resurrection and his victory over the world, they are affirming his lordship over the whole of creation, and they are putting their whole selves under his lordship.

The lordship of Jesus and the contemplation on the Kingdom

What does this have to do with the contemplation on the Kingdom that comes between the First Week and the Second Week of the Spiritual Exercises? The contemplation on the Kingdom sets up the whole Second Week, and together with the contemplation and meditations of the Second Week, it is meant to contribute to a conversion process that culminates in making a decision (the Election). The contemplation on the Kingdom has two preludes or preparatory steps. The first is to imagine "the synagogues, towns, and villages through which Christ our Lord used to preach." The second is to ask for the grace to be open and responsive to his call: "to ask the grace from our Lord that I may not be deaf to his call, but prompt and diligent to do his most holy will." Notice that Ignatius calls Jesus "Christ our Lord" and "our Lord." He does this habitually, almost always using the phrase "Christ our Lord," right from the beginning of the Spiritual Exercises.

The two parts of the contemplation suggest the content of the concept "Lord." The first part considers an earthly king whose "will is to reduce to subjection all the lands of the unbelievers," and who calls people to join him, sharing his hardships and life-style, working at his side. The second part applies this parable of the earthly king to "Christ our Lord." Christ, in contrast to the earthly king, stands as Lord of everything.

The first point of this second and, of course, culminating part of the contemplation on the Kingdom of Christ is "to see Christ our Lord, the eternal King, and before him the whole world." The universality of Christ's reign or lordship is indicated by the words "the whole world." Later in this same contemplation, he is called "the universal Lord" and "the eternal Lord of all things."

39

The retreatant is to hear Christ saying, "My will is to
conquer the whole world and all enemies, and thus to
enter into the glory of my Father. Whoever, therefore,
desires to come with me must labor with me, in order that
following me in pain he may also follow me in glory."

The second point considers that anyone who
has reason and judgment will make a total offering of self
for this enterprise. And the third point is to consider
that some will wish to go even further and to embrace
actual poverty and suffering of reproach, with Christ and
in imitation of him, if he chooses them for that.

To point out some likenesses and differences
between the lordship of Jesus Christ in the charismatic
renewal and in the contemplation of the Kingdom of Christ,
the first thing to note is that the Latin word for kingdom
(regnum) could also be translated into English as reign
or rule or lordship. So this contemplation might be called
one on the "lordship of Jesus." Second, it is precisely
Jesus as universal Lord who is contemplated. And – this
is another point of similarity between the concepts of
Jesus's lordship in the charismatic renewal and in the
Exercises – the initiative is clearly understood to be
with the Lord. It is he who calls, he who gives the power
to answer the call; the stress is on openness to grace,
on looking at the Lord and listening to his call.

There seem to be two marked differences. The
contemplation on the Kingdom (lordship) of Christ under-
lines the idea of giving oneself for the service of evangelization more than does the charismatic renewal's idea
of Jesus as Lord. Second, the contemplation on the
Kingdom places more emphasis on the desired generosity of
the person who is listening to the Lord, more stress on
making a total offering of oneself to the Lord to be with
him, serving him, in his work of saving the world. The
contemplation on the Kingdom asks the retreatant to *give
to the Lord* more *(magis);* it exhorts him to go further;
this is the idea of the *magis* that characterizes the contemplation and, as a matter of fact, the Exercises as a
whole.

In the charismatic renewal, on the other hand,
one may say that contained in the very concept of the
lordship of Jesus is the notion that whoever affirms Jesus

40

as Lord should *expect more from him,* precisely because he
is Lord of all things. The Lord is seen more as Giver
of gifts because he is Lord of all things, whereas in the
contemplation on the Kingdom the Lord is seen more as to-
be-followed-in-service. Hence the call to generosity.

The meditation on the Two Standards

A companion meditation to this contemplation
comes up on the Fourth Day of the Second Week of the
Exercises. It is the meditation on the "Two Standards,"
The two standards are two banners or flags, "the one of
Christ our supreme Captain and Lord; the other of Lucifer,
the mortal enemy of our human nature." This meditation is
a comparative consideration of the devil and all his demons
their strategy and tactics, and Christ our Lord, who calls
many and "sends them throughout the world to spread his
holy teaching among people of every state and condition."
Like the contemplation on the Kingdom of Christ, the meditation on the Two Standards finishes with a prayer to be
accepted, if it be the Lord's will, into his service in actual poverty and in bearing reproaches and offenses in
imitation of him.

Two parallels with the charismatic renewal
are evident. First, again, the lordship of Jesus is
brought out with emphasis. He is called the "Lord of the
entire world" as well as "Lord" and "Christ our Lord."
Second, the reality of the devil and of demons is, just
as in the charismatic renewal, taken seriously but quite
serenely. As well, the practice of "rebuking the devil"
is found both in the Exercises (the Rules for the Discernment of Spirits) and in many quarters of the charismatic
renewal.

The combination of taking Jesus seriously as
universal Lord and serenely accepting the existence,
malice, and activity of the devil is not accidental. The
danger of taking the devil seriously is a panicked flight
into some kind of Manicheism where God and the devil are
understood as equal or almost equal adversaries. This
danger is avoided, and serenity in the face of all the
forces of evil is attained, only when the *dominion* of God

41

is emphasized. As it is in the concept of the universal
lordship of Jesus Christ.

Prayer. As a conclusion we can pray, putting
everyone and everything and every activity - whoever and
whatever is significant in our lives, on our minds - under
the lordship of Jesus, explicitly placing each person and
each area of life into his hands and under his lordship.
And, in the spirit of the contemplation on the Kingdom of
Christ, we can look at Jesus risen, and see and hear him
call us by name to follow him, to serve him side by side
with him. Then, we can respond to that call by addressing
to Jesus the prayer of the contemplation on the Kingdom.

"Eternal Lord of all things, I make this offering with your grace and help, in the presence of your
infinite goodness and in the presence of your glorious
mother and of all the saints of your heavenly court, that
it is my will and desire, and my deliberate choice, provided only that it be for your greater service and praise, to
imitate you in bearing all injuries, all evils, and all
poverty both physical and spiritual, if your Sacred Majesty
should wish to choose me for such a life and state.

* * *

SERVICE AND PRAISE: IN THE EXERCISES,
IN THE CHARISMATIC RENEWAL, IN THE CHURCH

Both the Spiritual Exercises of Ignatius Loyola and the charismatic renewal have at the center of their attention Jesus Christ. The activities by which the retreatant making the Exercises and the participant in charismatic renewal are called to center themselves on Jesus Christ are, in both cases, praise and service. Here, I would like to make a descriptive comparison of praise and service in the Spiritual Exercises and in the charismatic renewal. This will lead to a brief discussion of those gifts that are called charisms.

Service and praise in the Spiritual Exercises

The first Principle and Foundation of the Exercises, the initial and basic consideration of the whole program, a kind of prologue, begins: "Man was created to praise, reverence, and serve God our Lord." After the Foundation, the retreatant works through his First Week to the contemplation on the Kingdom of Christ, which repeats the basic concepts of the Foundation, but understands them in the framework of the lordship of Jesus.

In many ways the contemplation on the Kingdom is a second Foundation. The prayer at the end of the contemplation speaks of "service and praise" of Jesus Christ in the context of offering oneself to him. Both in the Foundation and in the contemplation on the Kingdom, the retreatant is encouraged to seek what is toward God's *greater* service and praise. The Foundation concludes logically that we should seek, desire, and choose only what *most* fulfills the purpose of our creation: praise, reverence, and service.

In both exercises, service and praise are graces, gifts from God. Ignatius makes this especially clear in the 15th "annotation" or preliminary note for following the Exercises: "During the time of the Spiritual Exercises, when the soul is seeking the divine will, it is better and more fitting that its Creator and Lord himself communicate with the devout soul, inflaming it to love and praise him, and disposing it for that way of life by which it will best serve him for the future." Service and praise are our activities; but, in the first instance, they are the Lord's gifts to us that we may use them.

In the Spiritual Exercises, the words "service and praise" occur often, especially in the key exercises. In the medition on the Three Classes of Men, men of the third class seek only the Lord's will and whatever "seems to them better for the service and praise of his Divine Majesty." The phrase "service and praise of his Divine Goodness," as formulating the criterion of choice or decision, finishes the meditation. And the last words of the meditation on the Three Degrees of Humility are "service and praise of his Divine Majesty." In the prelude to making the Election, the norm for making important life decisions – the only norm – is "the service and praise of God our Lord and the eternal salvation of my soul." In the rules for the discernment of spirits, "service and praise" of the Lord is pointed out twice as a criterion for discerning whether an interior impulse or leading comes from a good or a bad spirit.

Both praise and service, then, are gifts from the Lord; they are the activities we were created for; and they are our response to the Lord's personal call. The spirituality of the Exercises calls not only for praise and service, but for *greater* praise and service, to praise and to serve better, in the best possible way according to the Lord's will and choice.

Most charismatic prayer meetings begin a prolonged period of prayer of praise. This may be followed
by teachings, prayers of petition, witnessing, and the
other common elements of such meetings. But praise occupies a key place.

What do I mean by praise? For one thing, praise
differs from thanksgiving. When I thank God, I show gratitude for his gifts and, in my prayer, I refer them back
to him in my thanks. But when I praise God, I give him
credit, so to speak, not for his gifts but simply for himself. I can praise him for his actions, for the things he
does, or I can praise him for his creation or for parts of
his creation; I can praise the Lord for anything and for
everything because he is the Lord of all things. I am not
thanking him precisely; rather, I praise him for being
the kind of Lord he is to have done these things, to have
created these things this way, to act as he acts.

Furthermore, by praising the Lord, I open my
heart to him; I take a stance of worship, going out to God
on his own terms, not for what he does for me personally

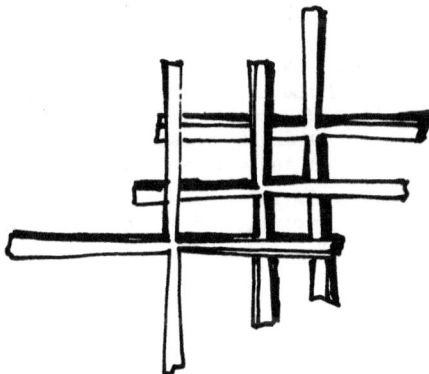

but for who he is. And in opening myself to the Lord through praise, I open the door of my heart to his graces and gifts; I become especially receptive to his Holy Spirit, who praises Jesus and the Father in me and through me, and in whom I offer praise to God.

The gift of tongues has praise as one of its chief purposes – a praise that has nearly no intelligible content except that it goes straight out to God on his own terms. And, like the gift of tongues, praise is a gift. People who are initiated into the charismatic renewal frequently find that they seem to have a new gift of praising God.

Praise has always been at the center of prayer in the Judeo-Christian tradition. The psalms are hymns of praise: some of them are almost nothing but praise. The psalms praise God for all creation, for his powerful saving acts in history, and for his own divine attributes. Even the psalms that cry out to the Lord in affliction often praise him from the midst of desperate situations. And the Christian liturgy, especially the Mass, is to a large extent praise. However, praise has rarely, in recent times at least, been as emphasized as it is in the charismatic renewal.

Praise and service, in the charismatic renewal, find their relationship within the framework of the gifts of the Lord. The purpose of God's gifts of grace is praise and service. When "the gifts" are spoken of in the charismatic renewal, what one ordinarily means is not the classical "gifts of the Holy Spirit" of the Roman Catholic tradition (Is 11:2-3; usually listed as wisdom, understanding, counsel, strength, knowledge, piety, and fear of the Lord), but rather the charismatic gifts, the charisms.

What are charisms? The word "charism" (from the Greek *charisma*, meaning gift) appears frequently in the Pauline writings. Sometimes it means simply a gift of grace, an effect or concretization of grace (e. g., Rm 1: 11; 5:15-16; 11:29; 1 Co 1:7; 2 Co 1.11). At other times, "charism" has the meaning that today's use gives it: a special gift, given to some but not to all, for the building up of the Body of Christ that is the Church. In this sense, a charism is a call to build up the community through some usual function and, at the same time, the means to fulfill that call. No one person has all the charisms, but the Body of Christ possesses them all, distributed among the members of the Body (1 Co 12:7). And the greatest charisms are those that are most efficacious for building up the community.

A charism, then, is a gift for service of some kind. Also, a charism is a new way, a special way, of relating to the Lord. It is a call to service (with the power to perform that service), and also a new way of being in relation to the Lord precisely in terms of that particular charism.

Charisms are of many sorts

What are some charisms? The most commonly cited list is that of 1 Co 12:8-10: "For to one is given through the Spirit a word of wisdom, and to another, according to the same Spirit, a word of knowledge; to another, faith by the same Spirit, and to another gifts of healings by the one Spirit, to another the working of miracles, to another prophecy, to another the discernment of spirits, to another different kinds of tongues, and to another the interpretation of tongues, and in all these things operates the one and the same Spirit." This list, of course, is far from exhaustive. Other lists of charisms can be found in the same chapter (12:28-30) and in the two succeeding chapters (13.1-3; 14:6; 14:26) as well as in Romans (12:6-8) and Ephesians (4:11). There is no complete list, and all the lists together do not seem to be complete.

Some other charisms besides those mentioned the list given above are: the gift of teaching, the gift of assisting, the gift of governing, and the gifts of almsgiving, ministry, exhorting, sharing, leadership, cheerfulness, evangelization, "shepherding." There is much overlapping in the various designated charisms, and a few are obscure as to their meaning. What they have in common is that they are all special gifts of the Spirit, even if some charisms have natural gifts as correlates (e.g., leadership, teaching, cheerfulness), and may be built upon nat-

47

ural inclinations. In these charisms, the Holy Spirit becomes, we might say, almost visible, audible, tangible; all the charisms manifest the one Spirit whose gifts they are.

Charisms have always been a part of the Christian tradition in one way or another. Every age has had its gifted teachers, its great religious leaders, its miracle workers. The founding and rapid spread of the Franciscans marked a great outpouring of the charism of evangelical poverty. There have always been those with the charism of missionary work (see Vatican II's document on the missions, *Ad Gentes,* 4:23), and there have always been many with the charism of consecrated celibacy (see 1 Co 7: 7, "I wish that all could be as I am, but each person has his own charism").

Charisms are referred to 14 times by Vatican Council II, years before there was a Catholic charismatic renewal. The most important passage is from *Lumen Gentium,* the Dogmatic Constitution on the Church (number 12; see also numbers 4 and 7):

"It is not only through the sacraments and Church ministries that the same Holy Spirit sanctifies and leads the people of God and enriches it with virtues. Allotting his gifts 'to everyone according as he will' (1 Co 12:11), he distributes special graces among the faithful of every rank. By these gifts he makes them fit and ready to undertake the various tasks or offices advantageous for the renewal and upbuilding of the Church, according to the words of the Apostle: 'The manifestation of the Spirit is given to everyone for profit' (1 Co 12:7). These charismatic gifts, whether they be the more outstanding or the more simple and widely diffused, are to be received with thanksgiving and consolation, for they are exceedingly suitable and useful for the needs of the Church.

"Still, extraordinary gifts are not to be rashly sought after, nor are the fruits of apostolic labor to be presumptuously expected from them. In any case, judgment as to their genuineness and proper use belongs to those who preside over the Church, and to whose special competence it belongs, not indeed to extinguish the Spirit, but to test all things and hold fast to that which is good (cf. 1 Th 5:12, 19-21)."

The use of charisms is what characterizes charismatic renewal. Not that charisms in the Church are restricted to the charismatic movement, of course. Even the gift of tongues, which seems to be one of the most distinctive characteristics of charismatic renewal – and the use of which is principally in personal (private) prayer – is found outside the charismatic movement as a gift given to some individuals for the building up of the Body of Christ in their private prayer of praise and of petition.

The chief use of many charisms is in communal prayer meetings. At almost any large charismatic prayer meeting, one can observe the charisms of prophecy, of teaching, of leadership, of exhorting, and of tongues – both in spontaneous group praise, and in prophecy together with the use of the gift of interpretation. However, the use of charisms as characteristic of the charismatic renewal is also found outside the context of prayer meetings, especially in the form of gifts of healing, of evangelization, and of tongues in private prayer; charisms are found in use also in counseling and similar situations, in the form of gifts of knowledge, of speaking wisdom, and of discernment of spirits.

Charisms in the Spiritual Exercises

Can we say that charisms are referred to in the Spiritual Exercises? Well, if we look in the Exercises for the charisms of 1 Corinthians, chapter 12, we will not find them. In fact, the Exercises put far more emphasis on the Giver of gifts than on the gifts themselves. The Exercises lead the retreatant to be open to all gifts, including charisms, and to desire to be in intimate relationship with the Lord; to desire the Giver more than the gifts, but to be ready to receive gifts and to desire them as ways of being closely related to the Lord.

On the other hand, there are certainly several charismatic gifts that receive special attention in the Spiritual Exercises. To begin with, the "actual poverty" referred to so often in the Exercises is, surely, the *charism* of evangelical poverty, given to those whom the

Lord calls to that kind of poverty. This is why Ignatius wants the retreatant to be open to that gift and ready to receive it if the Lord so wills – because it is a gift given to whom the Lord chooses, a charism.

The same seems to be true of "bearing reproaches"; the desire to suffer rejection and contempt with and for the Lord (all other things being equal), rather than the opposite, surely seems to fulfill the definition of a charism. Here again, Ignatius urges the retreatant not to work for the gift, but to desire it and be ready to receive it if the Lord so wills. Other charisms, although less central, are referred to in the Exercises: the gift of tears, for example, and the charism of evangelization.

A charism that has great importance, particularly for the director of the Spiritual Exercises, is that of "discernment of spirits." Ignatius gives two sets of rules for the discernment of spirits, one for those going from sin to sin, and the second set for those making progress in the spiritual life. Ignatius's rules for the discernment of spirits are squarely in line with, and are a high point of, the whole Christian tradition of the discernment of spirits, a tradition that finds its beginnings in the public ministry of Jesus and in the early Church (1 Co 12-10) and that still continues in Jesuit spirituality as well as in the charismatic renewal. In fact, there is no question but that the tradition of the Spiritual Exercises has much to contribute to the charismatic renewal regarding the use of the charism of the discernment of spirits.

Service and praise in the Church today

Both the Spiritual Exercises and the charismatic renewal present a Christian balance of praise and service as the way we give God glory and, at the same time, become close to him. Nevertheless, in at least many cases, the Spiritual Exercises seem to be interpreted today as giving a comparatively greater emphasis to the component of serice. And in the charismatic renewal, in many cases, the temptation remains to stress praise and to neglect Christian service outside the charismatic community. This can all be put in a historical perspective, with emphasis on recent history.

A Catholic leitmotiv of the 16th and 17th centuries was that we are created to give God glory through service and praise. This theme runs through not only the writings of Ignatius Loyola, but also those of Francis de Sales, Leonard Lessius, and many others. Later, especially in the 19th century, the idea of glorifying God through service received less attention from theologians than did the concept of praising God, of glorifying him through praise of his revealed glory. And so, Vatican Council I (1869-1870) solemnly declared that "the world was made for the glory of God." This must be understood according to the theology of that time: the "glory of God" includes both the glory that God gives to his creatures and by which they manifest his greatness, and also the praise that we should give God as a response to the manifestations of his greatness.

These two ideas were central in Catholicism in the late 19th and early 20th centuries. Nature and history show forth God's glory: "The world is charged with the grandeur of God; it will flame out like shining from shook foil," wrote Gerard Manley Hopkins, in his poem "God's Grandeur." And we are called to lift up praise to God, to glorify him in response to his glory that he reveals to us. Elizabeth of the Trinity wanted to be nothing other than "a praise of glory" (*Ecrits spirituels*, Paris, 1948, 203-204), echoing Hopkins's "Glory be to God ... praise him" in his "Pied Beauty."

Vatican Council II marks a change in the Church's understanding of how to give God glory. The emphasis shifts from praise to service. The first two chapters of that Council's Dogmatic Constitution on Divine Revelation contain a whole theology of the revelation of God's glory, a revelation that finds its completion and fulfillment in the risen person of Jesus Christ. It is the glory on the face of the risen Jesus, who is the Light of all nations, that radiates to all peoples and brightens the face of the

Church (Dogmatic Constitution on the Church, *Lumen Gentium*, 1:1).

This Christocentrism is repeated in the Pastoral Constitution on the Church (*Gaudium et spes*), but with a strong future-directedness, with a radically eschatological theology. The Introduction, especially, contains a developed theology of the universal lordship of Jesus Christ. It understands all reality as centered on the risen Jesus Christ and moving toward him as its Lord, its goal, and its future. The Introduction states that Jesus Christ, who died and has risen, is "the key, the focal point, and the goal of all human history" (no. 10). Later on, the document says: "Jesus Christ is the goal of human history, the focal point of the longings of history and civilization, the center of the human race, the joy of every heart and the answer to all its yearnings" (Part I, 4: 45). The same paragraph goes on to quote the New Testament regarding the Father's plan in Christ: "To re-establish all things in Christ, both those in the heavens and those on earth" (Ep 1:10), and the words of the Lord, "I am the Alpha and the Omega, the first and the last, the beginning and the end" (Rv 22:13).

Human progress, then, is in continuity with the world to come, even though human freedom makes progress often ambiguous; earthly progress must be distinguished from the growth of God's kingdom, but it is of vital importance to the kingdom of God. "For after we have obeyed the Lord, and in his Spirit nurtured on earth the values of human dignity, brotherhood and freedom, and indeed all the good fruits of our nature and enterprise, we will find them again, but freed of stain, burnished and transfigured. This will be so when Christ hands over to the Father a kingdom eternal and universal... On this earth that kingdom is already present in mystery. When the Lord returns it will be brought into full flower" (Part I, 3:39). And so "it is clear that people are not deterred by the Christian message from building up the world, or impelled to neglect the welfare of others. They are, rather, more strictly bound to do these very things" (Part I, 3:34). Thus the theological develpment moves from a theology of the lordship of Jesus to a spirituality of service in this world.

52

The most important Catholic theological contribution since Vatican II has been the Latin American theology of liberation.   The theology of liberation became a
broad, coherent movement with its own clear identity at
the Second General Conference of the Latin American Epis-
copate (CELAM) in Medellin, Colombia, in the fall of 1968.
Medellin sought to interpret the Latin American signs of
the times in the light of faith. What is Christian freedom as described at Medellin and in post-Medellin liberation theology? Christian freedom is freedom in the Spirit, but this interior freedom is not unconnected with social, economic, and political freedom. On the contrary,
the freedom that Christianity brings is freedom from sin,
and sin is often found in the very structure of human society as well as in the hearts of men.

Sin within the person has consequences in society, and so it comes about that situations arise which
are objectively sinful even though perhaps involving no
immediate subjective responsibility at the time that those
situations exist. Sinful structures, social, economic,
and political, do exist in society; they are objective
states of sin. Situations of unjust distribution of
wealth, of oppression of various kinds, of starvation, of
homelessness, of inhuman living conditions - all these are
sinful situations, conditions of institutionalized vio-
lence.

It is, then, essential to the Church's mission
to condemn such sinful social structures and to work to
overcome them so that people may live more fully. The
glory of God, for liberation theology, as for Ireneus, is
man fully alive. And the Church must strive to change
these sinful social situations that impede and obscure
God's glory.

Official Church teaching, like theology, has
followed a path of increasing emphasis on service as giving glory to God, on the Christian imperative to build a
better human future.

    -   In *Populorum Progressio* (1967) when speaking

of the Church's contribution to the development of man and of all men, Pope Paul said that what the Church has to give is primarily a *vision*, a global vision of man and of humanity.

Four years later, he approved the document *Justice in the World* drawn up by the 1971 Synod of Bishops. It speaks of the rights of all men and all peoples to development, of the fact that often economic, social, and political structures oppress man, and of the need for the Church to denounce injustice. It states that the Church's mission includes, as an essential element, not only a vision but *action* for justice.

The 1974 Synod of Bishops stressed that the Church, in its mission of evangelization, must announce the "integral salvation of man, his full liberation;" and asserted the need for Church action to liberate men from unjust social and political conditions as well as from their personal sins and sinfulness.

In my opinion, Catholic thought is moving now into a new phase. From the First Vatican Council until the Second, there was a certain theological neglect of the human this-world future. In a second phase, since Vatican II, man's earthly future has been somewhat overemphasized. Theologically, the trajectory has been from God-centered theology to man - centered theology - to what Karl Rahner calls "Christian anthropology."

But now, it seems to me, there are signs in Catholicism of a third phase, of a Christ-centered theology that does justice to both God's glory and man's this-world future. The tone of theology and piety can be seen shifting from the prophetic to something close to a contemporary apocalyptic. Sinful social structures are recongized not only as to-be-changed (prophetic), but as demonic and to be brought under the lordship of Jesus (apocalyptic). Hope in man, even hope in Christian efforts, is giving way to hope in the power of God and in Jesus as the only Savior. Hope in the future is understood less as what Christianity calls us to, and more as God's gift: "Christ in you, the hope of glory" (Col 1:17). God's glory is understood less as the future we build toward, and more as God's future that breaks in on us in the power of the Spirit of the risen and glorified Jesus.

Furthermore, service and praise are coming into synthesis as the twofold Christian response to God's revealed glory. "For it is the God who said 'Let light shine out of darkness' who has shone in our hearts to give the light of the knowledge of the glory of God in the face of Christ" (2 Co 4:6). The God who reveals his glory in nature and in history – for he is Creator of both – also reveals to us, in our hearts, his glory, the glory that shines in the face of the risen Jesus. And this fact, that the God of nature and history reveals himself to us personally, synthesizes those two aspects of Christianity that are codified in the phrases "glory of God" and "future of man."

My personal relationship with God who speaks to my heart in revealing his glory, on the one hand, and my relationship with the world in which I find myself involved, on the other hand, come into synthesis by reason of this great fact: the God of my heart is the Lord of nature and of history. The God I praise and pray to is the Lord not only of my future but of the future of mankind and of the whole world.

My "upward" impulse to praise and to union with God, and my "forward" impulse toward service and involvement in the world-as-the-future-to-be-built, are brought together. Because the God of the "upward" and the God of the "forward" are the same. They are the same Jesus risen, both God and man, who centers the whole world on himself and who reveals and radiates the glory of God. Jesus's revelation of God's glory, moreover, gives meaning to the future, not only to the ultimate future of the world to come, but to the immediate future of life in this world.

The great danger is that both praise and service can become formalized, empty forms, not truly actions of God's Spirit in us. For they are both primarily not what we do on our own, but God's gift to us. Service and praise are his gifts to us before they can become our gifts to him. All we can do is to remain open to God's gifts, with as much humility as we can manage, in the face of the glory that he reveals to us and of our own radical inability to respond to it except in the power of his Spirit.

* * *

FRANCIS A. SULLIVAN

WHAT CAN THE CHARISMATIC RENEWAL AND
THE EXERCISES GIVE ONE ANOTHER

I have sometimes asked myself why so many priests and religious are skeptical about the charismatic renewal. One reason, I believe, is the impression that the renewal claims to be some sort of shortcut to sanctity, or to be offering great gifts of the Spirit at "bargain prices," a kind of "cheap grace." In other words, what people are called upon to do seems too little, the effort they have to make seems too easy, to justify the results that are claimed by advocates of the renewal. Since it seems unlikely that the great graces that are claimed could be obtained in so easy a way, many presume that time will show the results obtained through the renewal were rather superficial after all.

I wonder if this does not reflect a tendency to judge the likelihood of our receiving a gift from God, or the value of the gift we might receive, on the basis of the effort we have to make to receive it, rather than on the generosity of God. Does it betray a mentality that thinks of grace as a reward for our efforts, rather than a free gift?

At any rate, I think it helpful to recall the parable of the workers in the vineyard (Mt 20:1-16), which shows that God may wish to give just as great gifts to those who have worked but one hour, as to those who labored from morning till night. If, then, the Lord chooses to pour out his Spirit in abundance in answer to a simple prayer made in expectant faith, who are we to say that this is too easy a way to obtain so great a grace?

Are the claims of the charismatics true?

I would suggest, though, *first*, that we approach this question simply on the basis of the evidence, without any a priori exclusion of the possibility that people may actually be receiving the graces they claim to receive through having been "prayed with for the baptism in the Spirit." Personally, I am convinced that there is more than enough evidence to show that God is really answering the kind of prayer that is being made in prayer groups of the charismatic renewal.

This does not mean, of course, that I am inclined to accept every claim that is made. Enthusiasm can no doubt lead to exaggeration, and a passing consolation can be taken as a sure sign of a lasting change in one's relationship with God. But in my view, great changes have taken place in people's lives in so many cases that I cannot doubt that God's Spirit is really being poured out in answer to prayer.

The *second* point I would like to make is that in fact there are some very strong elements in this renewal, which help to explain why it is so effective a method for leading people to an experience of genuine conversion.

The first such element is the power of the gospel itself, when presented in a simple, straighforward way by people who have themselves been grasped by the power of this message. I do not know where in the Catholic Church today the gospel is being more effectively presented, or people are being more effectively evangelized, than in the Life in the Spirit Seminars of the charismatic renewal. Perhaps we had thought there was no need to evangelize people who were already baptized Christians. But if we agree with Karl Rahner that there is need for a personal conversion in the life of the baptized Christian, then we ought also to see that there is no more powerful call to conversion than the simple message of the gospel itself.

The second element that I think helps explain the effectiveness of the seminars as a method of leading

58

people to conversion is the power of personal witness. An essential part of every teaching in the seminars is the testimony of the one giving the talk, as to how the Lord has moved into his or her life, and what changes this has brought about. The members of the team who act as leaders in the small-group discussions after the talk are likewise ecouraged to share their own experience of coming to know the power of the Spirit.

Such sharing takes place, not only in the seminars, but in the normal prayer meetings as well. Even the most carefully prepared and eloquent sermons can hardly match the effectiveness of this kind of personal testimony, as a way of leading people to believe that God's grace can bring about similar changes in their own lives, and to want to dispose themselves as best they can to ask for and receive such grace.

Where two ot three are gathered in my name...

The third element that I believe explains the effectiveness of the renewal is the power of the group, both to help people find a new life in the Spirit and to sustain them in that new life once they have found it. The typical prayer group in the charismatic renewal meets once a week for a meeting that is open to anyone who wishes to attend. There are many things about prayer meetings that people can find attractive. The atmosphere is typically warm and friendly; newcomers are made to feel welcome. There is usually a good deal of singing, mostly of lively songs that are easy to learn and that people enjoy singing. There is a variety of prayer, teaching, witnessing, and the like, which makes most prayer meetings quite interesting, so that even though they last an hour and a half or two hours, the time does not usually seem to drag.

Another important advantage of such prayer meetings is that if a person is attracted by what happens in them, and continues to come, he may participate at whatever level suits him. No one will put pressure on him to do anything he doesn't feel comfortable doing. He may continue at a rather superficial level of participation for quite some time. But the chances are that some day he will hear someone witness to what the Lord has done in his life – and it will make him want the same for himself. He may come to realize that Jesus is not really the Lord of his life the way he has come to be Lord in the life of that other person. And so he will enroll in the Life in the Spirit Seminar, the next time one is started.

Here again it is the group that will help him to listen to the gospel in a new way, and to open himself up to the grace that God wants to give him.. For it is the prayer group that provides the team that gives the talks, leads the discussion groups, and eventually prays for the outpouring of the Spirit on those who ask them to pray with them for the grace of a real conversion and renewal of their lives. And finally, the prayer group will provide ongoing support to help the person persevere in the new way of living the Christian life that the Lord has opened up for him by the gift of his Spirit.

Positive advantages of the renewal

So there are three elements in the charismatic renewal. They may seem rather simple, but they possess real power to lead people to conversion: the power of the gospel, the power of witness, the power of the group. In some respects these elements give the charismatic renewal advantages that the Spiritual Exercises do not have. For instance: the renewal has the advantage of being a popular movement, in which lay people have a key role of leadership. A great many prayer groups are formed and flourish without the need of a priest to get it started or to lead it. This has made possible the rapid expansion of the renewal in so brief a time, and the vast numbers of participants. Whereas the Spiritual Exercises require a trained director, usually a priest or religious, it is quite usual for the Life in the Spirit Seminars to be conducted by prayer groups that do not have any priest participating in them.

Likewise, the open prayer meeting has proved to be a strong factor for leading people eventually to want a deeper life in the Spirit, and thus to enroll in a Life in the Spirit Seminar. And nothing is a more effective way of leading people to want to make the Spiritual Exercises. Moreover, as we have seen, the prayer group provides the follow-up and support that most people need in order to persevere in a new life in the Spirit. How often the fruit of a retreat is dissipated and lost for the lack of such engoing support after the retreat is over!

Of course, the Spiritual Exercises have their strong points too, which I hardly need to explain to an audience like this. It is certainly not the intention of these lectures to try to prove that the charismatic renewal is a better method than the Spiritual Exercises for leading people to conversion. It is even less our intention to suggest that the day of the Spiritual Exercises is over, and that we should drop them in favor of the Life in the Spirit Seminars. I hope we have made it clear that we have nothing like that in mind. The purpose of these lectures is rather to compare these two different methods of leading people to conversion, to see what elements they have in common and what each might have to contribute to the other, and above all to see how a judicious combination of the strong points of the two might make both of them more effective.

Positive advantages of the Exercises

First of all, I would like to express my conviction that anyone who has come to know the Lord in a new way through the renewal could very profitably make the Spiritual Exercises. In fact, I would imagine that such an individual would very likely be just the kind of person that St. Ignatius looks for in the prospective exercitant: one, namely, who is ready "to enter upon them with magnanimity and generosity toward his Creator and Lord, and to offer him his entire will and liberty, that his Divine Majesty may dispose of him and all he possesses according to his most holy will" (Annotation 5). In addition, most of the people who come into a new life in the Spirit through the renewal really need the solid teaching and opportunity for spiritual growth that is available through the Exercises. For a great many, if not most, of the lay people who are the great majority in the renewal, being "baptized in the Spirit" is the very beginning of their spiritual life. Most of them have never before tried to make personal prayer an important part of their daily lives. Probably few of them have experienced spiritual consolation or desolation, and fewer know how to interpret and profit from such experiences. The gift of the Spirit has filled them with a great desire to "walk with the Lord" and to "live in the Spirit," but they still have a great deal to learn about what this means in the concrete. I do not know any better method for helping people to grow securely in the spiritual life than the Spiritual Exercises. And if this is true for the rank and life in the renewal, it is all the more true in the case of those who find themselves in positions of leadership in prayer groups. Frequently, such people receive real gifts of leadership and even pastoral direction of others, but there is obviously a great deal they also have to learn, if they have never had (as is very often the case) any professional training in spiritual direction. I would certainly encourage such leaders to make a retreat according to the method of St. Ignatius. Of course, it would be particularly helpful if the one directing the retreat were also involved in the renewal.

What the Exercises might learn from the renewal

If I were giving an Ignatian retreat, what elements, if any, would I introduce into the retreat from my experience in the charismatic renewal?

First of all, I would always respect the wishes of those making the retreat, leaving them quite free to decide whether they want anything of the renewal to be introduced into the retreat or not. (I presume that I would be giving the retreat to a group of people who are not already involved in the renewal.) If I found that they were open to something of the renewal, I would try some or all of the following.

Group prayer. I would suggest that in addition to the periods of private prayer, which of course would remain the essential elements of the retreat, there be a period of prayer in common each day, preferably in the evening. Many people are already used to some form of shared prayer; others might be willing to try it. I would encourage free, spontaneous prayer, especially of praise, adoration and thanksgiving, in preference to prayers of petition, although not excluding the latter.

Witnessing. In the context of such prayer, I would encourage the participants to share the personal reasons they have for praising and thanking God. This would introduce the element of witnessing, which has proved so powerful a factor in the renewal.

Prayer for inner healing. On this point I would follow the suggestions given above by Father Faricy, when he was explaining the meaning of such prayer, and its place in the context of the First Week of the Exercises.

Prayer for a new outpouring of the Spirit

I would explain why I believe we should pray explicitly, and with expectant faith, for such a new outpouring of the Spirit, and why so many have found it particularly helpful, when they are seeking such a gift, to ask others to pray with them and for them. Then I would suggest that a good time to pray in this way during an Ignatian retreat, would be after the contemplation on the Kingdom of Christ. The dispositions with which St Ignatius expects the retreatant to make the colloquy of that contemplation seem to me to be the very ones that people making the Life in the Spirit Seminars should have when they ask to be prayed with for a new outpouring of the Spirit. As we have seen, Fathers Flick and Alszeghy understand the month of the Exercises as "nothing else than a knocking, a seeking, an asking for the Spirit." Such seeking and asking could be all the more effective, I suggest, if they were done explicitly, with expectant faith, and with the concentrated prayer of the group for each individual who is seeking this gift from the Lord. I would expect the fruits of this prayer to be evident in the rest of the retreat.

Discovery and use of the gifts of the Spirit. One way in which the fruits of this prayer might be manifested in the rest of the retreat is that the retreatants would be more open to the gifts of the Spirit, both in their private prayer and in group prayer. Some might discover that they had received a gift of praying in tongues, and find how helpful this can be, especially in prayer of praise. The whole group might find a new freedom, spontaneity and enthusiasm in praying together, and experience how upbuilding such prayer can be. They might be led to pray for healing for one antother. Some might find that they were given words of ecnouragement, exhortation or consolation for the group, which the others too would find deeply meaningful and helpful. With the discovery and exercise of such gifts of the Spirit, the daily period of group prayer could become a more effective instrument for growth in the Spirit for all the retreatants. I would expect that the fruits of this would be manifested also in the daily celebration of the Eucharist.

But above all I would expect the fruits of the new presence of the Spirit to be evident in the ardor and devotion with which the participants made the rest of the retreat, and in their perseverance in the grace that was given to them in the course of it. To this end I would suggest how helpful it would be to continue to pray regularly with others who are also trying to live in the Spirit. I hope that this does not strike you as just a devious way of gaining recruits for the charismatic renewal! I will say simply that I know from my own experience how important, even how necessary I have found regular participation in a prayer group for my own perseverance in efforts to lead a spiritual life, and for this reason I heartily recommend it to others.

* * *